STARDUST AND YOU

Written by: Carol Gamble

Illustrated by: Sandy Vaillancourt

Text copyright © 2024 Carol Gamble.
Illustrations copyright © 2024 Sandy Vaillancourt.

All rights reserved. This book or any portion thereof may not be reproduced or transmitted in any form or by any means, electronic or mechanical, including photocopying, recording, or by any information storage and retrieval system, without written permission from the author. For information, address stardustandyou2024@gmail.com.

Printed in the United States of America.

Spark Initiatives L.L.C.

Introduction

You are made from stardust!

We are all made from stardust!

But what is stardust?

Stardust is a building block of life. We call these building blocks of life: **elements**.

You are made from the elements of life.

The very elements (calcium, carbon, oxygen and nitrogen) that you are created from were formed in an old dying star called a **supernova**.

Becoming aware of this truth awakens in you a new connection to the universe. It becomes a personal connection.

You realize you are in a relationship with the universe...

The stars in the sky gave birth to the elements that created you. You are directly connected to the stars in the sky.

Helping you grasp this exciting truth, that you come from the stars, is what this walk through time is all about.

So, take someone's hand and begin your walk, discovering together where the elements of life come from . . .

Our walk begins with the . . .

Heart of Mystery.

From the **Heart of Mystery** emerged...

photons, particles, antiparticles, and

intense heat.

Over time, the cosmos cooled just enough

for **hydrogen atoms** to form;

next came **helium atoms**.

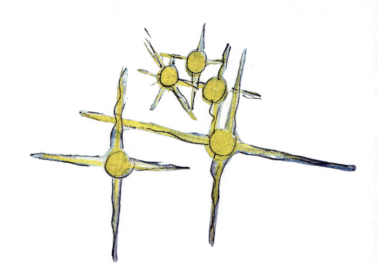

Over millions of years, **stars** were

born, matured, and died.

Years passed, and then . . .

It was time for **galaxies** to form.

Now, we come to one of the most MAGNIFICENT and AMAZING events in time...

called a **supernova!**

A supernova is a giant explosion of a dying star!

It is **extremely bright!**

It is **super powerful!**

When a dying star becomes a supernova . . . it explodes and spews out into the universe . . . the elements of life: calcium, carbon, oxygen and nitrogen.

These elements of life have been created in the star during its lifetime. These elements are the very elements that you are made from . . .

These elements of life are stardust!

YOU ARE MADE FROM stardust!!

SUPERNOVAS

Oxygen

Potassium

Calcium

Magnesium

Continuing our walk we come to our

Sun.

In a special galaxy, the Milky Way,

our Sun was formed

from the elements of . . .

hydrogen and helium.

Walking on, we find that it is now time for our

Solar System

to form.

Over millions of years, from the elements created in an old star and spewed out in a supernova explosion...

all the planets of our **Solar System** formed.

Now, we come to our planet

Earth...

Earth was created from

elements that came from the stars.

Earth has a special balance between all forces that allows life to come forth and flourish.

As we continue our walk we discover that

the atmosphere, oceans, lands, oysters, pearls, diamonds, fish, ferns, amphibians . . .

reptiles, flowers, mammals, and **YOU** are all created from **stardust** . . .

the life-forming elements that come from the stars!

Glossary

Atom: A tiny particle that is made up of even smaller particles called electrons, protons, and neutrons

Electron: One of three particles that make up atoms

Galaxy: A collection of thousands to billions of stars held together by gravity

Helium: A very light atom

Neutron: One of the three particles that make up atoms

Particle: Tiny bits of matter, such as electrons, neutrons, protons, and atoms, that make up everything in the universe

Photon: Particle of light

Planet: A large body that circles a star

Proton: One of three particles that make up atoms

Solar System: What we call our Sun and the planets that orbit it

Star: A ball of shining gas, made mostly out of hydrogen and helium, held together by its own gravity. Turning hydrogen into helium creates the energy that makes stars shine.

Stardust: The elements of life (carbon, oxygen, hydrogen, nitrogen) that come from the stars.

Supernova: A giant explosion of a dying star. It is extremely bright and super powerful. During a supernova explosion the elements of life (carbon, oxygen, hydrogen, nitrogen) are spewed out into the universe. These very elements of life were created in the star during its lifetime. These elements are the VERY ELEMENTS that YOU ARE MADE FROM!

Universe: Everything in existence -- all the stars, all the planets, all of space, elephants, giraffes, silver, flowers, trees, and YOU!

Inspired by:

Framer, Kim. *Happy Birthday, Universe! A Cosmic Curriculum for Children*

Swimme, Brian. *The Universe Is a Green Dragon*
  Bear & Co. Santa Fe, 1984.
  The Hidden Heart of the Cosmos
  Orbis Books, 1996.
  Canticle to the Cosmos
  Video Series

Swimme, Brian and Berry, Thomas.
  The Universe Story
  HarperCollins Publishers, New York, 1992.

Swimme, Brian, Sahtouris, and Liebes, Sidney.
  A Walk Through Time: From Stardust to Us -- The Evolution of Life on Earth
  John Wiley & Sons, 1998.

About the Author

CAROL GAMBLE

Carol Gamble is a mother, grandmother, entrepreneur, and a Montessori-trained educator; she is passionate about sharing the wonder of the natural world with young children. A young child's natural curiosity drives them to explore and discover the mystery of themselves, as well as the world around them. Creating special spaces for a child to explore and discover is critical for child development.

Carol believes *Stardust and You* is one of those special spaces for the young child to explore and discover, specifically, where the elements of life come from, fueling a sense of wonder that fills them with joy and awe.

Carol is also passionate about creating the right environment for each stage of a young child's development. Carol designed and brought to market The Original Learning Tower, an adjustable height step stool for toddlers. It provides a safe space for a young toddler to stand alongside their parent or caregiver at the kitchen counter, empowering them with independence. In 1992 Carol founded Little Partners to manufacture and distribute The Original Learning Tower. Little Partners continues to offer Montessori inspired children's furniture, including The Original Learning Tower, a variety of children's step stools, art easels, chairs and seats, climbing and balance products as well as toddler beds and storage products.

"If the idea of the universe is presented to a child in the right way, it will do more for him than just arouse his interest, for it will create in him an admiration and wonder, a feeling loftier than any interest and more satisfying."

-- Maria Montessori

"If a child is to keep alive his inborn sense of wonder, he needs the companionship of at least one adult who can share it, rediscovering with him the joy, excitement, and mystery of the world we live in."

-- Rachel Carson

About the Illustrator

SANDY VAILLANCOURT

Sandy creates watercolor, oil and mixed media paintings with a French Fauvism style. Living in Santa Fe, her work captures a southwest vibe with a French joie de vivre.

She was born in Northampton, Massachusetts, and studied art in California, New York, and Santa Fe. She received her MFA from Columbia University in New York City.

She became interested in art making in the late 1980s when her neighbor, a university professor of art in California, invited her to join her summer class. Her art has been featured on the cover of the Santa Fean Magazine and she has been part of the artist-in-residence program at La Fonda Hotel in Santa Fe, one of the city's oldest hotels, for the past 14 years. She is also the recipient of a the American Association of University Women fellowship. She is very interested in supporting children and teens in the arts and offers private classes in her studio in Santa Fe.

Made in the USA
Monee, IL
16 August 2025